Instructions in Joy

MEDITATIONS

Nancy Shaffer

Boston
Skinner House Books

Copyright © 2002 by Nancy Shaffer. All rights reserved.
Published by Skinner House Books, an imprint of the Unitarian
Universalist Association of Congregations, a liberal religious
organization with more than 1,000 congregations in the U.S. and
Canada. 24 Farnsworth Street, Boston, MA 02210-1409.

Printed in the United States

Cover and text design by Suzanne Morgan

print ISBN: 978-1-55896-424-2
eBook ISBN: 978-1-55896-633-8
6 5 4
15 14

Library of Congress Cataloging-in-Publication Data

Shaffer, Nancy.
Instructions in joy : meditations / by Nancy Shaffer.
p. cm.
ISBN 1-55896-424-X (alk. paper)
1. Religious poetry, American. I. Title

PS3619.H34 157 2002
811'.6—dc21   2002021155

With thanks to

Lisa, David, and Jo,

my teachers all,

and

the Unitarian Church of Davis, California,

that precious community that called out my Yes

Contents

Preface

The poems—meditations—gathered here were written for use in worship services, an ordination, a religious education class; for the comfort of friends; in response to spiritual direction, world events, seminary classes, and simple daily happenings. Many of them began out of my need to find words and form for joy; all of them began out of my longing to know a particular thing or feeling more fully. Each, in its birthing, has taught me something about joy, for if I listen well, poems come with a wholeness, a truth, a comfort I could not on my own invent: They hold beauty, even if they also hold anguish. Poems come to me as gifts. I offer them back as gifts.

Nancy Shaffer

Were I to Teach a Course on God

Were I to teach a course on God
I would begin with a plate of persimmons—
the sweet, crisp kind, the ones more
orange than red: the hard, squat Fuyus
I eat each November morning on hot
wheat cereal with almonds.

I would slice the persimmons gently
across their fat centers, then hold them
out. *See the star shape?* I would
offer them, so all might wonder.

I would slice brown Bosc pears
straight down their middles,
so the threads of each stem
trace wispily down to that rounded
place where dark seeds lie, tear-shaped
and wet in white, firm flesh.
I would hold these halves
silently forward, their bottoms smooth
in the curves of my palms.

I would teach God with plates of pomegranates,
both before they were opened and after.
I would bring wet washcloths.
We would bury our faces and eat:
all that luminescent purple-red,

those clear-bright kernels fitted in tight rows
on small and tumbling hills—
and all that juice, so easily broken, sweet
and puckery at once. We would say nothing.

I would teach this way:
with plates of fruit, a knife;
many washcloths. With my eyes
very large; my mouth mostly silent,
so all might eat.

In the Beginning

Kate is teaching the kids about dinosaur air.

"That air you breathe—that air
you have inside you every time
you take a breath—that's dinosaur air,"
she says. "Dinosaurs breathed it."

The kids' eyes are very wide.
They take deep gulps of air, just
to have more dinosaur air inside them.

"The air we have is all the air
we ever will have," Kate says,
"so we have to take good care of it."

The kids gulp less. Consider
the air already inside.

Kate tells more.
"Actually," she says, "we're all cousins."

The kids look at each other,
disbelieving, believing: "You?"

"We—*all* of us—" Kate says,
"way, way back, began as cousins.
Way back in the beginning."

The kids whoop, clap each other
on the back. For the rest of the day,
they savor air and call each other "Cousin."

In Stillness

I have been looking for the words that come
before words: the ones older than silence,
the ones not mine, that can't be found by thought—
the ones that hold the beginning of the world
and are never used up, which arrive loaned,
and make me weep.

Because We Spill Not Only Milk

Because we spill not only milk
knocking it over with an elbow
when we reach to wipe a small face
but also spill seed on soil we
thought was fertile but isn't
and also spill whole lives and only
later see in fading light how
much is gone and we hadn't
intended it

Because we tear not only cloth
thinking to find a true edge and
instead making only a hole but
also tear friendships when we grow
and whole mountainsides
because we are so many and
we want to live right where black oaks
lived, once very quietly and still

Because we forget not only what
we are doing in the kitchen
and have to go back to the room we were in
before, remember why it was we left
but also forget entire lexicons of joy and
how we lost ourselves for hours
yet all that time were clearly

found and held and also forget
the hungry not at our table

Because we weep not only at jade
plants caught in freeze and
precious papers left in rain but
also at legs that no longer walk
or never did, although from the outside
they look like most others
and also weep at words said once as
though they might be rearranged but
which, once loose, refuse to return
and we are helpless

Because we are imperfect and love so
deeply we never will have enough days
we need the gift of starting over, beginning
again: just this constant good, this
saving hope.

First Sabbath

Tell me: did you really rest?
You who made day and night
and sky that separated
waters above and below,
you who told the waters
below the sky
to stay in one place
and out of them
asked dry land,
who told the earth
to send out growing things
and then made sun
and moon and stars,
who made birds that fly
and everything that swims,
and cattle and all creeping things
and every animal untamed
and then made man and woman
and finally, supposedly, rested:
tell me: how—
in the midst of all that buzzing
and flapping
and slithering and stepping,
all that bursting forth of leaf
and fruit and stem
that never had known themselves

before—tell me:
how could you possibly have *rested*,
after seeing what no one
ever had seen before:
beak, hoof, pebble;
after losing yourself
in a thousand versions of blue:
water in sun,
sky against sky,
the horizon where
sky and water meet:
how did you shut your eyes,
how not keep
turning and looking?
Didn't you long to caress
each small thing—notice
how toes work, and
stamens, and fingers?
Weren't you hollering out in amazement?
Weren't you so filled up glad
you couldn't sleep?

Reception

Two women, thin, one small, one gray-haired,
sit side by side on a high-backed bench.
The smaller one leans against the other,
lays her head atop the other's shoulder,
wraps her arm around the other.
The one wrapped around, leaned against and
onto, sits upright.

The smaller one sits up also, but
cannot restrain herself: again leans,
again wraps. Still the other sits upright.

The smaller one takes her arm back,
her cheek back, the side of her body back.
Sits also upright. And so this dance
continues—only, look: it is not
a gray-haired woman and a smaller one.
Rather, a gray-haired woman and a boy,
twelve, an aunt and nephew, mother and son,
exuberance and angular reserve.

The boy—I cannot see his hand but
this is true: I see his shoulder—reaches
for the woman's hand. Never does she
reach for his or look at him. He tries
again, impossibly: leans toward, whispers,
wraps his arm around, lays his head.

Later, I see the boy, freckled and open-faced,
punch cup in hand, turning toward me,
limbs new, not yet his own;
taller than I imagined when sitting.

Oh, I say—almost say, grabbing after
my fingers, pulling my hand back, already
nearly outstretched—*Oh*, I say, almost: *whoever
taught you to love, you just keep loving.*

But he is gone. My words float away, unsaid.

These I anchor, send after him: *Gods who
dole out children, you keep him sturdy.*

And: *Whoever taught this child to love,
please, just keep loving him.*

Field at Table

When I begin to bless this food
and close my eyes I lose myself
first just in green: how
do leaves grow themselves this
green and how do they
grow at all to be so large and
how do they make themselves from
soil which in itself is only brown and
sunlight helps and water but
how is the end of this, *green?* How
can I bless this food? It blesses me.

Thank you, I say, for this bowl
which also is field, this green
which is meal before
I eat. *Thank you,* I say,
that this green becomes *me.*
Thank you for mysteries, this life.

Blessing for Bodies

May we creatures of bone and tissue
know our bodies well:
the fourth rib, and how it rises
higher than third, not so high as fifth;
how it feels to the thumb, slowly traced,
and under it, how the heart rests.
May we know that space where
no ribs lie, and unshielded, we bend.

May we know the bottom of each
toe, and that tender arch where
no skin touches ground;
also skin smoothed soft by clothing.

May we know the quick curve of the head
before it sits on the spine,
and the tiny hollow just behind the ear;
the length of the forearm,
lifting food to lips, and how lips become
a circle, waiting—and knowing this,
cease our study of war.

A Theology Adequate for the Night

Not God as unmoved mover:
One who set the earth in motion
and withdrew. Not the One to thank
when those cherished do not die—
for providence includes equally
power to harm. Not a God of exactings,
as if love could be earned or subtracted.

But—*this* may work in the night:
something that breathes with us, as others
sleep; something that breathes also
those sleeping, so no one is alone.
Something that is the beginning of love,
and also each part of how love is completed.
Something so large, wherever we are,
we are not separate; which teaches again
the way to start over.

Night is the test: when grief lies uncovered,
and longing shows clear; when nothing we do
can hasten earth's turning or delay it.

This may be adequate for the night:
this holding: something that steadfastly
breathes us, which we also are learning to breathe.

After a *Sacramento Bee* Report, May 30, 1999

I who am without a child and middle-aged
would like to adopt twenty young
ethnic Albanian girls, gang-raped in a basement
four nights straight by Serbian soldiers.
The girls' mothers and brothers, held above
at gunpoint, heard their screams.
Now the girls are dead to their families.
Some have been sent to join the rebels
in the hills. They will probably die fighting,
say their fathers, but that is better than living
defiled: they are not blameless.
Have dishonored their families.

I have been thirteen, eleven, fifteen,
twelve. I have walked long distances, but
not to hills after being raped. I have not been
gang-raped, and not for four nights straight.
I cannot imagine finding myself still
alive, after. Can imagine wanting to die,
all through the rapes: my body violently
stolen and broken open
and used as garbage heap, not once
but over and over and over, publicly,
with no possible way of resisting,
except to pray and keep on breathing.
I can imagine that terror,
that helplessness, that despair.

I can imagine being thirteen, walking
without knowing I am walking:
my feet somehow move, but nothing else
inside me: I am dead. My family believes
I am not blameless.

I want to adopt all these—children,
still. Want to let them rest quietly
in pale light in my small house, speak
or not as they desire, weep as they begin
it seems forever. I would bring them cantaloupe
and soup, let them sleep late;
find astilbe and lobelia in the garden.
I would put paints out and pencils
and clay, even rocks; invite ways of starting
to say what can never be said.
Would wash them and their clothing,
mend what I could; call in healers,
send the cat among them, innocent
and silken. Would open my arms
very wide; weep and pray.

Left

When those expelled from a land
set out carrying children and frail ones
and whatever other parts of their lives
their backs or heads or fingers can hold,
how do they walk upright not ten meters but
whole kilometers and then whole days? How
do they walk past wanting, past hope? Do they
speak to their bodies—tell their arms,
You must carry this, not drop this, not
put this down? tell their feet, *You must*
keep stepping, because I can't do this without
you? tell their necks, *You must stay tall,*
no matter the weight above, below,
behind? Do they implore each
cell to help each other one? Because
later, however much longer later is, hips
must bend to sit or fold to lie and then
stand up again and elbows, flex; knees,
lift: the ache and weight of journey must
not lock into bone, not pull muscle
from its lodging: no *after* can come,
except through this *now*.

This is why, finally, a small bundle is left
here by a tree; another, hours later, here

by a rock: the feet said they might continue
if the hands and back let go these things;
the hands and back said *Yes,* that everything
still living might yet live.

Offering for Grief

Look! I have made this bowl
for you, this large dark blue one
with lilies etched across the bottom,
around the sides.

I have cleaned this box for you,
lined it in soft brown wool.
Have set it here by the stove,
warm.

You could lie under the mulberry tree
at the edge of the garden;
wait in grass for lacewings and evening.
Or lie on the bed, light falling near.
Sit on the bureau.

What I mean to say is:
I will make a place for you.

Questions, Driving Near Dusk

Twice—on occasions about a year apart—he had asked
the same question: *Did God speak to just two people?*
Just Abraham and Moses? He had read this somewhere,
not in the Bible itself, which he hadn't read
cover to cover, but somewhere like *Newsweek,*
an article about God and prophets.

Ummm . . . she had said, both times, realizing
there was no answer he would not dispute.
I think God talks to everyone. Some people know it.
She added, *He talked to Jesus all the time.*
The question was impossible,
as if God had once been an actual person
and someone had been around to write down
everything He said, and then had been
able to get it copied into the Bible.
Why? she asked.

Well, what if they were lying?

What if who were lying?

The ones who said God spoke to them,
or the ones who wrote that down.
He did not turn to look at her as he said this.

Why would they lie? she asked, huffy now.
He thought the Bible was one huge hoax?

Not every time God talked to people got written down,
she told him. *Not everything that happened got put in the Bible.*
It was edited. People chose what got in.
She did not right then also take on
the matter of God's gender.

As before, he did not say what he really wanted to know,
and she did not know how to ask—for surely
this was something lonelier than a question,
something she had stepped into at the last minute.

What do you believe He did? she asked finally,
wanting to turn him upside down, like an hourglass
run out: something else, his own, should fall out.

Oh, I don't believe in God, he said,
so quickly she knew he had been waiting.

Oh—said softly, other possibilities too complicated,
night and trees now indistinguishable.

He was silent also, the thing at last said.

That Which Holds All

Because she wanted everyone to feel included
in her prayer,
she said right at the beginning
several names for the Holy:
Spirit, she said, *Holy One, Mystery, God*

but then thinking these weren't enough ways of addressing
that which cannot be fully addressed, she added
particularities, saying, *Spirit of Life, Spirit of Love,
Ancient Holy One, Mystery We Will Not Ever Fully Know,
Gracious God* and also *Spirit of This Earth,
God of Sarah, Gaia, Thou*

and then, tongue loosened, she fell to naming
superlatives as well: *Most Creative One,
Greatest Source, Closest Hope*—
even though superlatives for the Sacred seemed to her
probably redundant, but then she couldn't stop:

One Who Made the Stars, she said, although she knew
technically a number of those present didn't believe
the stars had been made by anyone or thing
but just luckily happened.

One Who Is an Entire Ocean of Compassion,
she said, and no one laughed.

That Which Has Been Present Since Before the Beginning,
she said, and the room was silent.

Then, although she hadn't imagined it this way,
others began to offer names:

Peace, said one.
One My Mother Knew, said another.
Ancestor, said a third.
Wind.
Rain.
Breath, said one near the back.
Refuge.
That Which Holds All.
A child said, *Water*.
Someone said, *Kuan Yin*.
Then: *Womb*.
Witness.
Great Kindness.
Great Eagle.
Eternal Stillness.

And then, there wasn't any need to say the things
she'd thought would be important to say,
and everyone sat hushed, until someone said

Amen.

Revision

As if it settles everything, he says,
"I don't believe in any old white-bearded
guy sitting up in the clouds." He stuffs his
hands in his pockets, fourteen and
slouching. I want to hug him into caring.

Instead I say, "What do you believe?"

"What do you mean?"

"You said what you don't believe in—some
'old white-bearded guy sitting up in the clouds.'
What do you believe?"

"I told you." He shrugs elaborately, hands
so deep in low-riding pockets his long
arms are not long enough.

At dinner I pass him fresh green beans, then corn,
rice as he likes it cooked with mushrooms.

He looks up. "Um . . . actually, there's more."

So, begins.

Last Learning

Mom, you say, *can't you just*
let go? and you do not mean
anything small like an argument
or an old hope or a sheet edge
she is holding, but also all of these
because she is dying.

Yeah, yeah, she says, flicking your
words into all the sky between
Florida and California, one of you
at each end. *Yeah, yeah.*

You ask because of the terrible
reason she is lucid today: unending
pain: she has climbed out of chasm
after chasm of medication to report this.
Is frantically caught between a body
far too ill with cancer ever
possibly to recover and
a lonely learning at the last minute
how to relinquish what remains.
She would choose neither.
Because she still can speak,
you hear in her very own words, formed
and not, this most anguished of suffering.

Mom, you say, loving her so much
you suggest her dying, *can't
you just let go?*

And all the sky between you,
you wait, engaging that *nothing* both
possible and everything: cradle her
with your voice: tell your love
which cannot end.

Afterward

Afterward, we want to say,
But can't we do that over?
Say, *But it was a mistake!*

Ask, wanting some other
answer: *It's forever?*

And sometimes, though all
light is slanted—as in autumn,
though it isn't autumn—
and all the earth lies tilted,
we cannot say the light is so,
the earth askew—for how
are we to live, how find hope,
if light itself is altered,
the earth not on its axis?

Grief is lonely in these ways,
begins in just such tearing: we were
nested in this earth; and now
are not. Knew this life by cherished
habits and have lost them.

Remembered One

If memory is not dream, mistaken
hearing, I have been remembering the girl
I heard about, young, who died from eating
her own hair. She had cut off some
part of it—from head,
underarms, legs—and afterward,
in remorse or perhaps in
panic, ate it. Her family
belonged to a sect that did
not allow cutting of female hair;
she longed to be like others, not
in their group—and died. Ingested
the evidence of her sin,
as if she might say, "Oh,
it's *not* shorter"—casually,
surprised—but died
for that hoping, her insides
strangled in hair. How
did she swallow it, how
chew it, how first think
no one might notice?

I know why she comes to me as
I trim the catmint plant,
contemplate my own hair,
stir wild rice: I am one who

survived. Cut myself off in
other ways; I did not die.

I want her to come back—
not dead all these years—
cut her hair as short as
she likes, pleased, laughing.
I want her to have lived to bear
children, care for others'
children, brush their hair long
into braids or run a comb
through it, singing and quick.

Mending

How shall we mend you, sweet Soul?
What shall we use, and how is it
in the first place you've come to be torn?
Come sit. Come tell me.
We will find a way to mend you.

I would offer you so much, sweet Soul:
this banana, sliced in rounds of palest
yellow atop hot cereal, or these raisins
scattered through it, if you'd rather.
Would offer cellos in the background singing
melodies Vivaldi heard and wrote
for us to keep. Would hold out to you
everything colored blue or lavender
or light green. All of this I would offer you,
sweet Soul. All of it, or any piece of it,
might mend you.

I would offer you, sweet Soul,
this chair by the window, this sunlight
on the floor and the cat asleep in it.
I would offer you my silence,
my presence, all this love I have,
and my sorrow you've become torn.

How shall we mend you, sweet Soul?
With these, I think, gently

we can begin: we will mend you
with a rocking chair, some raisins;
a cat, a field of lavender beginning
now to bloom. We will mend you with songs
remembered entirely the first time
ever they are heard.

We will mend you with pieces of your own
sweet self, sweet Soul—with what you've taught
from the very beginning.

For Margaret, Who Fights the Same Battle Over and Over

Listen:

When you quarrel with God
really you are quarreling with
those who have come after God.
It is not God who taught you only
a certain prayer or said reward
lies in only one direction. It's not
God who said *reward* rather than
embracing love, which is everywhere;
not God who taught you to hate
God, shun God. Those like you—
two-legged and mortal—did this: those
also hurt, in turn, by others before them.

You could leave off this quarreling:
just begin again, with just yourself
and God. You can choose a different
name for the Holy; stop cringing when
I say mine. Each is only a word for what
can't be said, the barest beginning,
a glimpse. The rest you may do in private.

But see, what you do there in private
shows: what you come back with is written
all over you. It doesn't matter

what the particular word is. Only
that you have been there to fetch it.
Only that you return there often, opening
yourself to everything that makes it.

Those who taught you what to pray and
how to pray were wrong, if what they
taught you, you hate.

You can begin again.

Pieces of Good

Rosemary tells us about power.
Thirty years ago, my friends and I
protested against the war in Vietnam.
It didn't make a bit of difference.
The war ended, but not because of anything
we did. We were powerless to affect that.

She looks carefully at each of us,
her words ringing. Has told us,
Scratch me and I'm Catholic;
believes in mystery and grace.

She nods at Darrel. *You were there.*

Darrel agrees the war was going to end
anyway.

I'd do it again, says Rosemary, *but*
it didn't make a bit of difference.

The class is silent.

I believe no piece of good is ever
lost, I say, no word an extra.
Everything offered toward good
makes a difference. Do not
say the detail of how I know,
which is all of my life: small love

begets eventually the large and whole;
finds itself in company with other
love set loose in the world.
The pattern emerges after, but
was always in the making.

Rosemary looks at me long.
Lets my point stand.

Later, Rosemary tells us
the story of Nien Cheng, who was
arrested and imprisoned and tortured
during the Chinese Cultural Revolution,
who pasted small squares of toilet paper
on her dirty prison cell wall to make a clean
space for her back to lie against.

That's personal *power—power from
within,* says Rosemary.

Nien Cheng used part of her
ration of rice to make the glue.
Survived.

Plain of Water

Since [she] held firm to her beliefs,
she was drowned in January 1539 . . .
  —Sigrun Haude, writing about
    Dutch Anabaptist Anna Jansz

My mother is driving a white car fast
around curves. First we speed through
a tunnel, then over a narrow road that
crosses a plain of water. My mother
loses control, the back end of the car
swerves out over the water, and while
my stomach becomes nothing and my
heart does not beat, the car tilts
upright, and we sink: long car;
flat, grey-blue water; brown road
just higher than water: from outside
the car I see this. I am also still
sitting inside on the car's back seat.
All is sudden, no one to save us.

Then what was air is water, sun
reaching down into dark green. I see
other cars, caught, silent; take
some comfort: we are not the first.
Then I understand I will die if I can't
make my hands unfasten the seat belt,

can't then roll down the window, find
air, the way up. My mother says
nothing. I wake, not dead, my body
breathing, closer in the night to those
whose sinking, bound, was not dream.

Hauling Out Stones

Once, he said an odd thing:
Forgiving begins with someone
sitting near.

Later, he said, *It isn't for the one*
who did the hurting.
It's the other one who needs it.

One day, without warning,
he wept.
I sat close.

He told an old hurt
in half-sentences and single words
like stones he was coming upon, new;
like tree limbs, broken,
which he needed both arms for hauling aside.

A half-dozen times that summer we sat,
he weeping, hauling out stones,
gathering limbs; I near.
The stones got smaller,
his sentences, longer.

He said, *It's the crying part*
I couldn't do by myself.

And later he said, *I feel cleaned out.*
A wan smile.

Still later, he said,
I think I've done it.

Made a kind of peace, he meant.

He slapped his palm hard against mine.
Laughed. Slapped his palm again.

Neighbors

I am running in my own apartment.
I paid the rent; I can do what I want.
I never want to speak to you again.
My neighbor spits this at me, each
word tight, voice a saw's edge.

I had gone up to say, *When there is*
running here, it shakes my whole
apartment. Can you please stop?
A friend had been trying to read aloud.
She could not concentrate, nor I hear,
for the noise and shaking.

Before my neighbor slams the door
I see his teenage daughter sitting
silently on a low chair; his young
son, wide-eyed, standing.

Meanwhile, a Swedish TV cameraman
is shot dead in Afghanistan by a bandit.

How to Tell Anguish

The fields are devastated,
the ground mourns . . .
                —Joel 1.10

You don't tell it all at once.

Consider Joel. Joel tells anguish in
pieces. He doesn't tell how one
certain person dies in famine after fig
trees splinter and sheep wander, dazed:
he tells that the wine is gone, the grain
is gone. Names only later precious
other trees that wither,
droop: pomegranate, palm, apple;
still later says that seed shrivels
in soil dried out to clods. Tells this
after locusts steal and eat, vines
wither, ground itself grieves.

You can't say anguish in any
linear way. It comes out in pieces.
My cat got ill. Someone hit my car.
My uncle sent a package. I myself
am ill. I am writing a paper.

No one lives a linear life.
Some construct it so, after.

You who know otherwise circle
around the hardest pieces. Maybe
say them only once, carefully fitting
details you don't tell elsewhere: *My friend*
tried to kill herself, you say. *In the garden.*
I'm having trouble getting my car's bumper
repaired. I found her.

Witness

To that place before words know
how to say themselves or
thoughts have an inkling they will be born

to that quiet place where the holy dwells—
that place before knowing,
stillness before form

where tears cannot stop—can find no
ending—and crying-out fills the sky

also to that place where the earth first
turns, and—turning—turns to bounty,
and we stumble upon hope

out of love, out of longing, you come.

Prayer for This Church

May each one among us have skin that longs to touch
other skin: fingertips that long for other fingertips
or whole hands and even arms; bodies that
want to stand next to other bodies, not alone,
while singing and bending, stirring soup.
May ones whose skin doesn't cry out for other
skin wish it did, and so teach it, so that no one
stands alone and no one aches and does not say so.

May our doors be so open it is drafty inside,
and people sometimes shout because noises without
come also within. May those sheltered here
sometimes cry, all at once, letting tear
water clean what words by themselves cannot.
In silent times, may every one present hear
every one else breathing, and know this is not
separate from how the world breathes all night.

May we always have enough room for those
many who want to come in. May those who cherish
this church be so glad they cannot stop speaking,
stop asking, and may that crowding itself be a gladness
as we keep adding rooms. May we notice
each one who is new and invite her to stay.
May our list of names for the Holy not ever
be finished; and may we hear God chuckling
with us as we find still more.

Calling

When you heard that voice and
knew finally it called for you
and what it was saying—where
were you? Were you in the shower,
wet and soapy, or chopping cabbage
late for dinner? Were you planting radish
seeds or seeking one lost sock? Maybe
wiping handprints off a window
or coaxing words into a sentence.
Or coming upon a hyacinth or one last No.
Where were you when you heard that ancient
voice, and did Yes get born right then
and did you weep? Had it called you since
before you even *were*, and when you
knew that, did your joy escape all holding?
Where were you when you heard that
calling voice, and how, in that moment,
did you mark it? How, ever after,
are you changed?

Tell us, please, all you can about that voice.
Teach us how to listen, how to hear.

Teach us all you can of saying Yes.

On Leaving Home

Leaving, I have wanted also
a *going toward*: something that
catches me on the other side.
Wanted not just *leaving* but
arriving.

So I have been grieving.

I form relationships with things:
the height of doorways, plum-colored
wool at the edge of a weaving,
the way shadows fall at night
and still I can see. I am anchored
by the physical: muse for what is within.
Move as I move, because of such holding.

It is not enough to say, *Well,
I am going toward God.*

There must be particulars—
a bright blue cloth beside a window
beside acacia; loved arms
of the human sort; deep wells of knowing,
only guessed at before.

This Making of a Whole Self

This making of a whole self takes
such a very long time: pieces are not
sequential nor our supplies. We work here,
then there, hold up tattered fabric to the light.
Sew past dark, intent. Use all our thread.

Sleeves may come before length;
buttons, before a rounded neck.
We sew at what most needs us,
and as it asks, sew again.

The self is not one thing, once made,
unaltered. Not midnight task alone, not
after other work. It's everything we come
upon, make ours: all this fitting of
what-once-was and has-become.

Footpath

I have made friends with a footpath, called by
its silence and age, how it lies steeply between one
winding street and the next. I come at dusk from
house-crowded streets to this hushed passageway.

The footpath tilts subtly left and then right
all down its length, never more than two
successive steps slanted in one direction.
The path has lifted, as earth beneath it lifted;
has cracked, all other possibility long taken.
Moss grows on step edges chipped by winter,
weight of feet. It arranges relationship:
has found soil enough, water enough,
enough light. It dares live in this middle—
possible, but unexpected.

The silence is that held time before knowing,
that filled time prior to worded thought.
In it, I am held all through my stepping,
in my pauses: am apprenticed through
my limbs to inventiveness, patience.

Overhead, pyracanthas bend, their branches
one single cloud. Birches bend, and hawthorns,
silk oaks, and magnolias, darker than the darkening sky,
shelter to this secret: by the blackberry and lily,
in shadowed licorice fern and ivy,

in steps old and cracked, out of plane,
a labyrinth is laid, a prayer to walk:
the soul to learn by bone, the bone by soul.

Still the Moon Increases

Trust is completely paradoxical:

The thing with which to begin when
you have nothing.

The end point, which
somehow you must find first.

The smallest of present moments,
measured haltingly into a past.

Both question and answer, when every
word of your acquaintance has fled.

You think the arc of the horizon
should split, one side jaggedly askew,
one forever gone.

The horizon doesn't split.
Its edges remain.

You think the ocean should dry to sand because
all the tears it held, you have used up.
You have stolen water even from the clouds.

But the ocean is not dried, nor the clouds
gone, though you have cried them both,

multiplied, and more.

You rub your eyes that grains still ripen,
plums turn blue, still the moon increases.

You thought all of this was gone.
Such is the unimaginable you have lived.
You thought everything was gone.

iii

But,
without your doing, the world is fashioned
in this way: moments
become other moments; steps
lead somewhere; all things breathe,
even without remembering.

One day, after a very long time,
without rubbing your eyes you see
the arc of the horizon still
an arc; the ocean, full.

And you are not betrayed, but glad.

Alchemy

That distillation of soul—which,
of all possessions, is most precious—
comes, if we are faithful,
out of sorrow.

This is the gift with which we
escape, stumble out:
we know the essence of this life
and who we are.

Ever after, whatever we have,
we have enough: begin complete,
even with nothing, even though
aching. In our lifetime we learn this,
while still we can cherish. Come
complete to the end, and are full.

Unitarian Universalist Meditation Manuals

Unitarians and Universalists have been publishing prayer
collections and meditation manuals for more than 170
years. In 1841 the Unitarians broke with their tradition
of addressing only theological topics and published *Short
Prayers for the Morning and Evening of Every Day in the Week,
with Occasional Prayers and Thanksgivings.* Over the years,
the Unitarians published many more volumes of prayers,
including Theodore Parker's selections. In 1938 *Gaining
a Radiant Faith* by Henry H. Saunderson launched the
tradition of an annual Lenten manual.

Several Universalist collections appeared in the early
nineteenth century. A comprehensive Book of Prayers
was published in 1839, featuring both public and private
devotions. Like the Unitarians, the Universalists published Lenten manuals, and in the 1950s they comple-
mented this series with Advent manuals.

Since 1961, the year the Unitarians and Universalists consolidated, the Lenten manual has evolved into a
meditation manual.

For a complete list of meditation manuals, please visit
www.uua.org/skinner/meditation

Also by Nancy Shaffer

While Still There Is Light
Poetry and Writings from a Minister Facing Death

A heartrending and heartwarming account of Nancy Shaffer's final year as she came to terms with her impending death. Part journal, part meditative poetry, and fully honest, Shaffer's account of her journey through denial to peaceful acceptance will lend inspiration and courage to those in need, and insight to those who give pastoral care.